OVERCOMING

IN

WAITING

Hope Built on Nothing Else...

Elohor T. Okoro Ayinmide

Published in Nigeria by:

Forte-Hold Publishers,

Ibadan, Oyo State Nigeria.

Printed By:

Elohortex Business Concepts, Adeyemo Alakija, Victoria Island, Lagos Nigeria.

+234-803-724-9986, +234-705-552-1750

elohortex@gmail.com

Dedication

This book is dedicated to God Almighty, for in Him I receive mercy and strength to life.

To those who are trusting and looking unto God for the recovery of their divine mandate your face will radiate with His Glory!

SPECIAL RECOGNITION

In loving memory of my dearest father, Andrew Okoro who passed on to glory to meet with his creator (14th of August 1955 – 1st November 1987). Although from human calculations your time on earth was short, notwithstanding, it was a fruitful life indeed.

You were well spoken of by family and friends and was popularly known for your hospitable personality and friendliness. The leadership role and family love that you showed for everyone to see and enjoy, is unforgettable.

Your commitment to standing up for the oppressed was remarkable. This is why as your children, we have continued in your legacy of true love that you genuinely displayed in the Spirit of truth, integrity, compassion, loyalty, faithfulness and empathy towards humanity.

The fatherly vacuum you left in the hearts of your children could only be filled by God.

Continue to Rest in the bosom of the Father! We love you but God loves you more.

Rest on Momento!!!

Also, in loving memory of my paternal grandpa, later Chief Peter Ekuemukpavwe Okoro, 1923 - 27th of January, 1983.

Acknowledgement

I want to express my gratitude to all my parents in the Lord who continue to pray for my wellbeing God will reward you openly, Thank you for all your support.

To my Provincial Pastor Olukayode A. Pitan and all Ministers in RCCG Tabernacle of David (Province 46), To my dear Area Pastor Ejimofor Akah and Pastor Phillip Odiavbara and all Temple of Praise (Area 001) Ministers, thank you for being there and allowing me to bloom where I was planted. To dear Pastor Elvis Onojeghuo and all Ministers in Praise Tabernacle Parish, and dear Pastor Thomas Akindeko and all Ministers in House of His Glory Parish, God bless you!

To all my friends in the vineyard, TOP House Fellowship Unit, TOP Fruitful Vine Fellowship, TOP Women's

Fellowship you all are wonderful! To dear Pastor Lanre Sunmonu who contributed chapter 11 and all Ministers in Transformation Power Evangelical Ministry. To dear Pastor Yemi Bakare and all Ministers in Early Church Pentecostal Revival Ministry. To dear Pastor Opeoluwa Awoniyi founder of Spiritnet Mentoring Center thank you and God Bless you all for your prayers and support.

To all my dearest siblings who are always at my beck and call, thanks for your wisdom and understanding.

To ERITAI FOUNDATION for her specialty and humanitarian service to the less privileged, God bless you for all you do!

To all my lovely cousins who stood by me when I needed their help, you are remembered for your kind-heartedness. God bless you all!

Thanks to all my uncles and aunts who were there to support me in their various capacity.

To my dear brother Sonni Atse, Sister Joy Agbaye, Sister Glory Aghoghovbia, Sister Harriet Arubi and dear Sister Blessing Boma Green God bless you all for lending your shoulders to lean on.

To my Chairman, bosses and the entire staff of Berkeley Groups Nigeria Limited. God bless you!

To all our staff in Elohortex Business Concept and Halleluyah Food Kitchen, you all make a wonderful team! God bless you abundantly.

To my loving husband and father of our children, Ige Ayinmide, who showed up just when I was rounding up with this book; I say thank you darling, for your simplicity and godliness.

To my dearest mother who ensured that my upbringing was her priority; a true disciple and disciplinarian whose actions molded my personality even to this day. Thank you, darling`meh'for your support.

To my ever-ready editor, Tryspect Solutions who edited the entire work and made it presentable, God bless you and your team.

Contents

Foreword

When Elohor told me to write the forward to this book, and I saw the title, I said to myself, this looks like one book with good promise. I am a lover of catchwords and titles, maybe it is because I do a lot of copywriting for organizations.

Then after, out of my busy schedule, I took out time to skim through the work, as I wanted to just read a chapter or two before closing it and continuing another day.   But once I picked this book and started reading, I discovered there is a message that I needed to receive from the book without delay. I discovered that God has truly given this young lady a message for the end-time Christians who are going through very difficult times of their lives and are contemplating giving up.

Daily, every single one of us come across situations that sweep us off our feet. At this stage, we begin to deliberate alternatives that do not necessarily go in line with the things we have before now believed in.

However, one thing that must be mentioned here is that your level of faith-building, before the difficult times rear their ugly heads, can go a long way to determine your stand with God in this difficult time. It also goes a long way to determine if we keep faith in this period or not.

What is really striking about this book is how Elohor opened her heart to share her experiences without shying away from important personal details. This book exposes us to the fact that nobody, no matter your level of spirituality is excluded from those tough times in life.

Citing very apt Biblical examples of great men, she discusses in detail how any believer can overcome in the face of trial and temptation.

'Waiting' for me, after going through this piece took a new meaning, and I knew that as a believer and follower of God, there is nothing that happens in our lives thattakes God by surprise. He is not called the Alpha and Omega for the aesthetics of the words. He indeed is the beginning and the end, and the author of this book went the extra length to show it.

I want to encourage anyone who is at the verge of giving up hope, who has stayed patient in the Lord all through the trying time and is considering giving up, I want to advise you to read this book. It will change your perspective about this journey that we are all in as believers.

This book couldn't have been written at a better time than this. In the face of the pandemic that has ravaged many in the different parts of the world, this is the book that will add some light to their lives, and help them to reach their victorious end.

Dickson Ekhaguere

Director of Creative Services,

Tryspect Solution

Testimony

This testimony is the account of God's faithfulness to His children and I recommend to you, dear reader, as a living epistle, to read it in the life of our sister, just as the scripture says that our lives are written epistles.

This story of Overcoming in Waiting is a confirmation of the word of God in our sister's life as a specimen of God's faithfulness.

To wait on God, you must be willing to close down all alternatives to God and burn the bridges behind you.

There is never a time that we are not waiting on God for one thing or the other, and claiming His precious promises. The message is timely; the lessons are life-time lessons and are deployable daily. Waiting proves that our sufficiency is of God.

For I will not leave thee, until I have done that which I have spoken to thee off.

Gen. 28:15

God's sincerity is established through such an amazing covenant unto Jacob.

Waiting on the Lord is one of the many paradoxes of life. Waiting physically is like a pause, but spiritually, it is speed.

But they that wait upon the Lord shall renew their strength; they shall mount up with wings as eagles, they shall run, and not be weary; and they shall walk, and not faint.

Is. 40:31

Waiting on the Lord is the demonstration of our absolute surrender and loyalty to Him. Our waiting expresses our dependency on God. God is as reliable as

His promises; in fact, Jehovah Himself is the ability that never fails.

Our waiting speaks to the mystery of God's faithfulness. Waiting is a difficult season because, during this period, the devil will always come to advertise several other beautiful alternatives to God's.

The secret to a successful waiting is understanding "THE FAITHFULNESS OF GOD." His faithfulness to His precious promises is the subject of our waiting on the Lord. Your waiting is to prove God's faithfulness.

Why will you wait on the Lord in tears, dried throat, failed eyes (Ps. 69:3) except you judge Him faithful that faithful is He that calls you, who also will do it. (1Thess 5:24).

You can only wait on Him as your defense (Psalm 59:9) because you have no other option. Many do wait on the Lord, but do it in the flesh, and so cannot tarry long. When others wait, they set time for God, and when their set time elapses, their attentions are shifted away from God to other attractive gods.

Many Christians have aborted their seasons of waiting because they lack the understanding of the mystery of waiting, which anchors on God's faithfulness.

Your attitude in waiting can determine how long your waiting time will be. If your attitude is so bad and carnal, then a journey of 13 days could take you forty years.

For those that wait upon the Lord, like Sister Theresa here:

Kings shall be their nursing fathers and Queens their nursing mothers. Is 49:23

- The Lord is good to them. Lam 3:25.
- Their change will come, they will overcome eventually. Job 14:14.
- God shall strengthen their hearts. Ps 27:14.

- God will take away their shame and their wheelchairs. Ps 25:3/ Ps 69:6.

- God shall give them their due inheritance. Ps37:9.

- In God shall be their hope. Ps 39:7

- Their expectation shall come from God. Ps 62:5/Ps 104:27/ Ps 145:15.

- They shall find mercy in the Lord. Ps. 123:2.

- Waiting is the path to obtain the promises. (Heb. 6:12).

Lanre Sunmonu (a.k.a. Lone Crusader)
Pastor and Founder,
Transformation Power Evangelical Ministry

Introduction

My faith in the Lord is strengthened every day no matter what the situation may be, because I have decided to stretch my faith beyond the limit and to break forth into the realms of victory. I have been encouraged to encourage others who are waiting and seeking strength in their times of despair; receive strength!

Experience has shown me that you are far better when you speak healing into your life even in the face of a paralyzing sickness because when you fall you will certainly rise again. So, don't stay down. Your heartfelt needs and yearnings will manifest if you don't faint and throw in the towel.

Because I trust in the Lord, even when his promises over my life have not yet manifested in the physical, I am always confident that he is working behind the scene. I have been encouraged by the word of God and the people God has orchestrated to build my faith. I never doubt God because I know He will always bring his promises to pass in my life (Psalm 118:8).

Waiting on the Lord is a must for every Christian especially when they are going through difficult times. In the timeframe between waiting and actualization, you must understand that preparation, training and planned actions must be carried out to make us better believers.

The conviction that waiting for the things which we will not be able to get by the work of our hands and our abilities unless God's divine intervention takes place, is enough reason not to be bound by trivial worries and occasional drawbacks. The Holy Bible tells us that we should be anxious for nothing, that in everything through prayer and supplication we should make our request known (Philippians 4:6).

In this book, you will understand the significance of waiting, and you will learn from the examples of those who have gone through very challenging times, both from the Bible and from very recent. I did not also shy away from telling my personal stories and experiences which I believe will motivate you and rekindle your faith in the Lord.

In everyone's life, waiting can actually be a difficult season. For example, let's assume you have been waiting for six hours for you to be attended to and the same thing you are waiting for, others have received theirs except you, certainly you will feel frustrated, pained and even envious of others. I can still remember when a particular bank was going under, due to some government policies that the bank could not cope with; and it was back then when I was still in the University.

The news of the shutdown had not spread yet. My neighbor in the hostel who knew someone that worked in the bank informed a few of us about this shutdown.

Very early the next morning, we rushed to the bank, but we discovered we were not the only one's privy to the information.

The queue at the bank was very long and the atmosphere was much tensed. After a while attending to a lot of people on the queue, the bank staff then told us they were stopping at that point and that the rest of us could return another day. But when we got there the following day, the bank had already shut down totally. I was beyond devastated. I lost a good amount that period, especially for a student.

Waiting can be really depressing when you have no hope of success in the end. It can be very frustrating, disappointing and worrisome. It might lead to a feeling of despair and denial. This has made many of us fall out of the place of our devotion because it is not an easy task. However, God has promised us that His Grace is sufficient for us (2 Corinthians 12:9).

Remember the book of Ecclesiastics 9:11 which says "I have seen something else under the sun: The race is not to the swift or the battle to the strong, nor does food come to the wise or wealth to the brilliant or favour to the learned; but time and chance happen to them all"

For your request to be answered, you must have a desire and the faith that your request will come to pass. Not complain, murmur or allow yourselves to be in a depressing desperate state that causes undue distress and sorrow. I am happy you have picked this book because this book will teach you all you need to know about waiting, it will encourage you and ignite you on how you can engage your mind and allow God's will to be done; because His Grace is sufficient for you.

The Bible tells us that David encouraged himself in the Lord (1 Samuel 30:8). God has promised you that it may tarry, but it must surely come to pass. Enter into His rest and stay connected as you read this book

"Overcoming in waiting; My life, My story" Hope Built

On Nothing Else.... God bless you richly.

Elohor T. Okoro Ayinmide

Chapter One

WHAT DOES IT MEAN TO WAIT?

You cannot deny there has never been a time when you thought you needed something so desperately but it wasn't forthcoming, and so you fret, lost your cool, felt frustrated or disappointed and maybe even depressed. We all witness that undecisive moment in our lives and for some, it happens more frequently: That point in your life when you believe if you do not get it, it would have been better you were dead.

Sometimes it could be simple things as waiting for the food to get done, especially when very hungry, or waiting for a mail to come in. Other times it could be as significant as waiting for a connection to work out a job position for you, waiting for the government to implement the demand of the citizens, waiting for marital breakthrough or even for the fruit of the womb.

Whatever the case, waiting is not an interesting time for anyone. Even the toughest and most persevering people wouldn't want to always find themselves in situations where they have to wait.

"WAITING" according to the Oxford English dictionary means the act of staying or remaining in expectation. Other definitions will also include "Attendance and service". For many of us who have attended parties before, also popularly referred to in the western part of Nigeria as Owambe, the people we casually refer to as servers, are the waiters in the party.

Their job is essentially to wait on party-goers and serve them food and drinks. Or let's take that of a restaurant, the waiters have a single job of standing by you until you make your order; these are the service or attendant service they perform. Meanwhile, I am not writing about restaurant waiters or party servers, it still however filters down to waiting on something or someone.

Based on the first part of the earlier definition of waiting given by the Oxford dictionary, which refers to waiting as the act of staying or remaining in expectation, what strikes me the most in this definition is the fact that waiting is first an ACT, and secondly an EXPECTATION. The last time I spoke with a church friend of mine about waiting, she tried to define waiting as "to be patient". But I quickly corrected her by letting her know that patience is only an aspect of waiting. Waiting is an act and an expectation.

An act means the process of doing something, while expectation means the act or a state of expecting or looking forward to an event as about to happen. Therefore, waiting means "to engage yourself in service while looking forward to an event you hope to happen or are waiting for". On the other hand, to be PATIENT means not losing your temper or cool while waiting. Now you understand why I said that patience is only an aspect of waiting.

To buttress further, the word you will most likely be hearing when you are going through hardship will be patience. People will tell you that for you to be able to come through with the solution to your problem you will need to be patient.

Patience, as they say, is a virtue and the few who have it have mostly attained good results. But in some other circles, I mean those who are not given to being patient, they will always cite the adage that "the early bird gets the worm" as a replacement for the adage that says "a patient dog eats the fattest bone".

What they are actually trying to achieve is to infer that you should not wait or delay, rather that you should try to go for something as soon as you can. But I can tell you for free that when you rush in, there is the likelihood of you rushing out.

In fact, that quote of "the early bird" has actually put some in more trouble rather than help them because the statement preaches impatience instead of patience. Fortunately, or unfortunately, the age we are in is a technological age where everything is fast and running. As a result, the idea of the patient dog no longer hold sway for many, especially young people. Let me actually bring these two lines of thoughts 'the early bird" and "The patient dog" into a unified perspective by using the word WAITING.

Waiting is DOING (early bird) while being PATIENT (the patient dog). Waiting is engaging your hands while still maintain your cool. It is that bird that knows that being in a haste to be the first will not always bring you the result, and it tells the dog that being patient doesn't mean you shouldn't wake up early. So, it integrates both sides, and that is why waiting is a very important asset everyone must possess, especially in difficult times.

The inability to grasp the concept of waiting has been the undoing of many and this has sadly resulted in making dangerous hasty decisions and leading them to make the wrong moves. We always think that we need something at the time we want it and because of this, we are caught up in dire situations that put us into more dangerous situations.

Our constant desire and haste with life is always gearing us to do what we shouldn't do, and want what is dangerous for us. Our mortal flesh will always make everything seem like a need for us and therefore we are always urging ourselves to get it as soon as possible, even when it doesn't seem right. No wonder the book of James says that our desires put us into trials and temptations (James 1:14)

Chapter Two

THE TWO KINDS OF WAITING

Basically, there are two kinds of waiting. There is the "waiting on the world' and "waiting on the Lord". Although the focus will be on waiting on the Lord, however, it would be worth it to expand briefly on the idea of waiting on the world.

Waiting On The World

I grew up in Delta state and only moved to Lagos Nigeria after completing my University education. While I was about hitting age 30, it was as though marital relationship wasn't part of my destiny. I am beautiful, virtues and academically savvy. But then, the kind of men that were approaching me didn't really fit into what I'd call men with strong personalities, neither were their demands pleasing to me. Did I pray?

Certainly, I prayed devotedly, was dedicated to God's affairs and never left the sight of God. Meanwhile, all those that one would assume as worldly were finding the men of their dreams, things were going so smoothly for them, well, I wasn't living with them so I couldn't tell if they had challenges. But from where I was standing, it seemed I was the only woman in the world that was having a problem deciding on a man.

I consulted books, attended marriage seminars, went for prayers and kept my hope on God even though it was taking longer than I would have wanted. It got to the point a good sister of mine who lived in the United States of America, although not sister by blood but is much more a sister than blood could have made us; she decided to wade into the matter.

She told me to hold on for her as she was mobilizing effort and resources to find me a very decent and comfortable man in the U.S who would marry me and most likely take me to the United States. If I must confess, nothing excited me more than the thought of finding a life mate with roots to the United States. It was a promise that made the world a bit better for me.

This sister wasn't someone who did not keep to her promise, she was somebody that I could readily rely on in the toughest times of my life and she wouldnot disappoint me. True to her word, she found someone for me, my only role was to get a visa and move to the United States.

As God would have it, I was denied the visa twice even when I thought I had met all the requirements necessary to pass the process. In fact, to make matters worse, this man in question refused to travel down to Nigeria for reasons best known to him. It was as if everything was working against my meeting this man, and consequently, we could not start a relationship. To say this negatively affected my emotions and made me felt unwanted is an understatement. But God had better promise for me.

In the world, there are many factors that are just waiting to crash your hopes and frustrate your efforts. Sometimes it may not even be the kind of disappointment like in my story, it could be worse, say the person that made the promise could just be taken by the cold hands of death. God forbid this is our case.

These kinds of disappointments can bring untold devastation beyond words and can be very sad and upsetting for anybody. You will then realize candidly that the most reliable man in the world is not reliable enough, and as long as he is clothed in mortality, he cannot control the factors of life and is susceptible to failing you. You will realize that men are prone to failing and disappointing you no matter how strongly established they are.

Waiting on the world means waiting for or asking a man to bring your heart desires to pass, as seen in the book of Genesis 30:1 where Rachel who was waiting for the fruit of the womb, decided to blame Jacob for her predicament. Hear what she said "give me a child or I die". Instead of praying to God for the fruit of the womb, she decided to rely on her husband, a human being, to grant her heart desire.

Don't get me wrong, I have seen occasions where men helped men rise from grass to grace. But again, if God does not put your help in the hands of a man, he cannot help you. Men are built to fail. Their biological composition influences everything about them just as their environmental, emotional and mental compositions affect them. Usually, if a man is not benefiting from what he or she is giving you, the likelihood of their passion for you to achieve success is very rare. If he, however, finds out that your success is going to affect his position or raise you to be higher than he is, there is the chance of him or her thwarting your dreams and sabotaging your goals.

Waiting on the world also means relying on your ability to bring to reality all that you desire. This can be readily seen among very talented and wealthy people who most times believe talent and money will always solve their problems; but from several scenarios, we have seen that just talent, hard work and money can only do so much, the rest is still on God to bring one desired success.

For those who have decided to rely on men and material things to realize their hopes, these people have already failed even before they begin their journeys. Waiting on man is setting your mind on what men can do for you. Men have very limited capacity and capabilities and they are always looking for what they will gain from you rather than what will benefit you.

For those who put their trust on man, when they are disappointed what usually set in is anger, aggression, pain, sorrow and the likes, because there is no succor in man. You would wait all you want, and while waiting you will still face the tragedy of penury. And after they disappoint you, you will still face even worse pain.

In Jeremiah 17:5-6 the Bible says 'Curse is the man who trusts in man and makes flesh his strength, whose heart turns away from the Lord. He is like a shrub in the desert, and shall not see any good come. He shall dwell in the parched places of the wilderness, in an uninhabited salt land."

Let me clarify this verse, it is important for you to understand that this verse is not God placing curses on anyone who relies on man or who has his high hopes rested on man; instead, it is only telling you the result of such an action. He is just stating the obvious fact about such a foolish mindset.

If the Bible says whatever you sow you will reap, it is not a curse, God is only telling you what happens when you sow, and the fact is that whatever you sow is exactly what you are going to reap.

This is what the book of Jeremiah is telling us, that such a man who relies on the flesh is "...A shrub in the desert, and shall not see good come". A shrub needs water to grow, therefore it is required that such plant is situated in a place it can easily draw water. But when the Bible tells us that it is a shrub in the desert, we do not need more details from the Bible about the sorrow of such a shrub.

Whether in waiting or the final close of its waiting, the Bible says it shall not see good come. As I have earlier stated, this is not a curse, it is a fact. Why wait on a man when his limitation even gives him a lot of trouble. Why depend on a man when you can depend on God.

A newspaper article reported an incident of a man who was duped of over 3million Naira in a job scam. He was to pay a total sum of 6million Naira but was first expected to make an initial deposit of 3million Naira, and after he would have received his employment letter, he was to pay another 3million Naira.

This young man would have been very hopeful and trusted that his moves, a 3million Naira move was good enough to help him secure the job position. His trust on the world to help him realize his goal of getting a job with a highbrow government establishment was exactly what the Bible described as "shrub in the desert..." that will wait in unexplainable penury yet "shall not see good come" because there is no succor in waiting on the world. Naturally, we are configured in a way that we want to see what we are relying on. We want to see the proof in what we are relying or waiting on that it can settle our problems.

Therefore, we are looking for those who have lots of money, who have web-like connections to top places and those who have the physical strength to do and undo. Once our eyes set on these kinds of people, we throw our trust in their words and promises. We wait and act according to their instructions believing that whatever they had promised us will certainly come to pass. Beloved, why be a shrub in the desert when you can flourish by the waterside, by the living water?

Waiting on God Alone

Having looked in detail on waiting on man and its unending tragedy, now it is time to get down to the real reason why you picked this book in the first place, and that is WAITING ON GOD. What does it mean to wait on the Lord? To wait on the Lord is to rest in the confident assurance that, regardless of the details of the difficulties we face in this life, God is our only anchor of confidence and rest. It means trusting God and trusting God only.

The word WAIT incorporates hope, anticipation, to be patient and to trust. To be hopeful and trust in the Lord requires faith, patience, humility, meekness, long-suffering, keeping the commandment and enduring to the end. To wait upon the Lord means planting the seed of faith and nourishing it with great diligence and patience.

It means waiting on the promises of God to be fulfilled. In the book of Matthew 6:10; Luke11:2 Jesus prayed to God our Father saying; "Thy kingdom come, thy will be done". Biblical waiting takes our mind to the sign on GOD's waiting room that reads 'Be still, and know that I am God' (Psalm 46:10 KJV). You can be still because He is active. Waiting is not the time to assume the worst, or worry, or fret, or make demands, or take control, because God is the one in control.

Although waiting is not inactivity, waiting is however a sustained effort to stay focused on God through prayer and faith. To wait is to rest in the Lord, and wait patiently for Him... not fret; God is the great physician. Waiting is the training process of God to become what He wants us to be. A time to act on your faith. God never leaves his children without a sure defense.

He understands that sometimes we fret in the face of unfamiliar troubles and challenges, but like he told the panicky Israelites trapped at the red sea by Pharaoh's army, "The Lord will fight for you, you need only to be still" (Exo 14:14), He is also telling us to be still and he will fight for us.

Chapter Three

WAITING IN TRIAL AND TEMPTATION

Through trials and temptations, our faith is tested always. It is these trial and temptation that determines the strength of our waiting. There will probably be no need to wait if there were no challenges. As long as we are in this world, there will be trials and tribulations, both spiritually, physically and mentally. Waiting is a trying moment in itself; it is a period for everyone who is believing God to intervene and manifest the needs of their heart.

These needs could be a deserved promotion at the office that you have been denied, you are going through a seemingly unending period of singlehood, prolong health problem like the woman with the issue of blood, a painful widowhood or a divorce, or could even be that your visa application has been rejected countless times, what about a student seeking for admission into the university with many years of fruitless effort and a government that will not pay attention to citizens welfare.

Temptation and trial are bound to arise in every human life, but it is what you choose to do with them and during the period that will determine the outcome. David chose to fall into the temptation of an adulterous act with Bathsheba but Joseph chose to flee from fornication by running away from his master's wife, and in the end, he was greatly rewarded.

Yes, it was clear that both David and Joseph had to face the music of the decision that they made, but you and I know that Joseph was on his way to destiny while David was going through penances by correcting an error that he had made for his destiny to be restored (Psalm 51).

The period of trial and temptation is either God trying to tell us something, or the devil trying to take something from us. Whichever it is, what we must never do is withdraw our faith and our trust from God. We must not let any of such alter our righteous standing with God almighty because he alone can bring the solution to whatever we face.

The time of trial and temptation is in fact a great time to draw even closer to God and seek his intervention. James 1:12 says "Blessed is the man who remains steadfast under trial, for when he has stood the test, he will receive the crown of life". For us to have a good grasp of this chapter, it will be imperative for us to understand that there is a marked difference between Trial and Temptation. The book of James helps us understand the difference between Trial and Temptation.

BE AWARE YOU ARE WAITING

James 1:2-3 says "count it all joy, my brothers, when ye meet trials of various kinds, for you know that the testing of your faith produces steadfastness'. By this verse, we can understand that a trial is that situation or moment God uses to test and draw us closer to Himself. When God sees the need to increase a man or a woman, He tries him or her to know whether that same man or woman will be able to handle the glory ahead.

On the other hand, James 1:14 makes us see the difference between trials and temptation when it said 'But each is tempted when he is lured and enticed by his own desire." This basically states that we receive temptation when we are lured by the things, we see others have and therefore want to have it.

We are tempted when the devil understands that we have an ungodly urge for something and therefore would want to present it to us just so that we will fall to his devices. The book of James also went further to say in James 1:13 "Let no one say when he is tempted 'I am being tempted by God", for God cannot be tempted with evil, and he himself tempts no one".

We see clearly that God does not tempt his children to sin. In fact, it is Satan the devil that tempts the children of God to sin. The devil deliberately takes things from us to make us fall into disgrace due to an inability to wait on the lord to intervene. We must also be aware that an individual can go through what by our earlier explanation can be termed,

Trial and Temptation at the same time. This is the event where God is involved in the process of our testing in order to crown you with higher glory like the example of Job (Job 1:6-12). As God's children, we can fall into any situation, whether being tempted by the devil or being tried by God, but irrespective of that, one thing the Lord expects and requires of us is to wait on Him who can make all things beautiful in His own timing. Waiting When the Enemies Strike

We know that the devil never rests on his oars and therefore constantly besiege us with all sought of attempts to test our faith and our ability to wait on the lord. The life of Job will help us understand better what it means to wait on the lord in trials and temptation. I mean when God permits the devil to test you while He watches, hoping you will wait on Him to the end, that we can safely call trial and temptation.

Job was a man who had enjoyed and seen life in its fullness. All he needed he got; he was living his dream life. The peak of it was that he knew God and God acknowledged him as a righteous man (Job 1:1). Though Job's temptation and trials were divinely orchestrated this is what some of us should come to terms with, that some of the challenges we face are not all caused by the foundational problem as it is commonly believed.

Like Job God gave the go-ahead, note God does not permit evil, God only wanted promotion for His son, knowing God's will and purpose for your life is the key to your manifestation. It was left for Job to make his choices either to yield to the temptation or win over it. God knew Job will not disappoint Him. If you know your righteousness is in Christ Jesus, you will understand that many are the afflictions of the righteous but God delivers him out of them all (Psalm 34:19).

The friends of Job including his wife asked Job to curse God and die, they believed the storm will not be over. Job had a relationship with God, that intimacy made Job to choose life.

Beloved, do you know God? The knowledge of God in Job made him not to yield to their counsel. 1Corinthians 10:13 says "No temptation has overtaken you except what is common to mankind. And God is faithful; he will not let you be tempted beyond what you can bear". But when you are tempted, he will also provide a way out so that you can endure it.

When the people close to you tell you that your problem cannot be overcome, there is every possibility for you to fall to such counsel. But God promised in the above scripture that He will make a way of escape, and that way in most cases is the grace to persevere.

During the critical seasons of my life, entering into what I call a deceptive relationship that almost made me lose my stand with God and almost overshadowed God's glory in my life, I understood the true meaning of trial and temptation.

On one occasion during the relationship, I was asked, knowing fully that I am a born-again Christian, to pass over the blood of a ram that was poured on the two-entrance doorpost of the family house as a ritual to their idol. It was New Year's Day.

I asked why I must do it, it was plainly explained to me that it is for the protection of the family. I told them it was against my Christian belief and contrary to the blood of Jesus that I believe is superior and more potent to protect me than the blood of a ram. I refused to undergo that ritual and as a result, I had to battle with rejection for not accepting to obey the family traditional rituals. Irrespective of that, I took my stand for what I believed and I knew that for every decision, you must be ready to embrace the consequence.

Our prayer daily should be Jehovah show me the way that I may not stumble in my step-in life, that even though I stumble may your infinite mercy find me and restore me to your path for my life! From Job's story, you can see that God is faithful and He rewards those who scale through the trying seasons of their lives.

BE AWARE YOU ARE WAITING

I encountered a Christian sister that God brought my way some years ago during a difficult episode in my life. She had a similar experience which led to a split from her husband. Now a divorced single mother, she had to work extra hours to sustain herself and her son. She rededicated and devoted herself to the service of God in this new season of her intimacy with God, seeking God's face for a second chance.

One day an old friend of hers who was also married, approached her for an adulterous affair. Even though she was going through a very tough time especially financially, she held on to her decision not to succumb to it because the word of God is against it and she believed in the faithfulness of God to restore her. Not too long after that incident, she got an invitation to travel to America with her son, and today she is happily married living the life of her dream.

There is a story I would like to cite here of Judah and Tamar (Genesis 38) because I have heard some people argue it almost out of context. This is a story of a young lady in the Bible that felt deceived in her waiting season. To her, she felt that waiting for the young man promised to her by her father-in-law to grow up for her to marry him and raise children, didn't seem achievable. So she went ahead and devised a means to get out of her season of waiting irrespective of the detriment that this plan may cause to her.

Pretending to be a harlot for her father-in-law to take her in, she succeeded in her plan. Practically she would have been put to death by that single act. She ended up being justified because it was promised to her she will marry the younger son of Judah after her husband's death which seemed to have delayed longer than expected.

This story in the scripture is not to tell you that you should devise a fleshly means that is against God's will, because you might not survive the consequence. Someone advised me some time ago why not just forget this marriage thing and just get pregnant for any man that comes your way.

I understand she said this from the viewpoint of time not being on my side. I saw that the word of God was contrary to this viewpoint even though I did weigh the option. I now know better that this was a test of my faith. Are you going through some tests and trials of your faith? Beloved of God, just hang in there, God will come through for you today in Jesus Name!

God alone can orchestrate some things to happen for a purpose, the lesson from Tamar's story shows God's mercy to all sinners and how He alone can turn our ugly story to a beautiful one. If it helps to mention here that God feels your pain, please understand that He does and He cares.

In the words of the old spiritual," Nobody knows the trouble I have seen; nobody knows but Jesus." What are you waiting on God for that is almost making you yield to Satan's counsel? Wait on God for His good thought concerning your life to come to pass because it will surely come.

He said in His word that even the captive of the Mighty will be delivered! Dry bones will rise again! He can do what He says He will do! With God all things are possible! Don't give up on God, don't give up on yourself! God will never give up on you. The Psalmist says the mercy of God which is His Love, endures forever. Nothing is too difficult for Him (Jeremiah 32:27)

Waiting When God Tries Us

"David said to Gad, I am in deep distress. Let me fall into the hands of the Lord, for his mercy is very great;

but do not let me fall into human hands" (1Chronicles 21:13). Unlike falling into temptations of the enemies who have one single goal of destroying us, God tries us in order to take us to a new level of grace.

There are some situations where God can ask us also to do the undesirable in our sight, but God's intention is to portray and bring forth a lesson to our generation to prove the expression of His love. This should be as a result of your close intimacy with God to hear Him. Like in the case of Hosea God commanded him to marry a harlot; this was well orchestrated by God (Hosea 1:2 and 3).

We should take note of the fact that it is not all waiting that is the oppression of the enemy, waiting can be orchestrated by God to train His children to actualize purpose that will bring a profound manifestation of His Will and Glory upon us. The Heavenly perspective comes as we focus not on the circumstances but the Lord and His Word.

God made Sarah wait, it has been prophesied In Genesis 17:15-16 that she will be the mother of all nations but this did not manifest as at when Sarah expected it to happen.

Rachael also waited until God opened up her womb to bear children (Genesis 30:22) Then God remembered Rachel; he listened to her and enabled her to conceive. Stop the human timing and allow God's timing to tick in your life. By so doing your waiting will not have a pressing pressure on you. The one that owns the time and the season is in charge of your life.

Listed below are more biblical examples of people who waited on God and they waited the right way; revert

The Shunammite Woman – In 2kings 4 the story of the Shunammite woman was a place of rest right in her predicament. She demonstrated contentment and satisfaction even though she was in need of a child, she and her husband never allowed their situation to bother them, and they were contented and they also went about their life and enjoyed every moment until God intervened.

When it seems God has pinned you into a corner in that desired expectation, we have the opportunity to set aside our human viewpoint and wait upon the Lord to show us His power, His mercy, His purpose and His salvation. Don't pause your life because a particular expectation has not manifested yet.

Elizabeth the mother of John the Baptist – Elizabeth was going about her life with her husband serving God in truth and in spirit. Physically and medically, the human timing for her had passed, but God came forth for her and gave her a son to be reckoned with. Her circumstances did not dictate to her and she served God alongside her husband. Elizabeth and her husband were anxious for nothing. It should be observed that God doesn't work with the human calendar, timing, medical prognosis, facts and statistics; He works and remembers us at His own timing and when He thinks we are ready to receive the special package from Him.

Manoah and his wife – They were both going about with their work when God remembered Manoah's wife. Prior to when God remembered them, they did not allow their childlessness to deter them in any way.

"A certain man of Zorah, named Manoah, from the clan of the Danites, had a wife who was childless, unable to give birth. The angel of the LORD appeared to her and said, you are barren and childless, but you are going to become pregnant and give birth to a son" (Judges 13:2&3). That was when baby Samson showed up.

We all know the impact of this young powerful and the strongest man of his generation. Beloved, Ask God to give you the strength to face trials and temptation because you must always remind yourself that it is always to the glory of God, and your upliftment.

Chapter Four

TRIAL AND TEMPTATION ARE OUR TRAINING GROUND

An effective training is one that integrates both the theoretical aspect and practical aspects of the learning process. Although no one graduates from life's school until death, but if you want to graduate from one level of glory to a higher level of glory in the realm of grace and God's abundant supplication, you will always face trials and temptation.

These are the training God takes us through to consider us for promotions. When we enter the training process, it helps us to form good character in Christ. Once we keep our focus on God during this trying time, our perception about circumstances begins to change as we are not focusing on our strength and abilities but trusting God who had called us into His marvelous light.

While we wait, God creates something special for each of us as promotion package. While we wait, we begin to learn things we have not before then understood or learnt. Some of us begin to gain unusual abilities and skills. Considering the life of Noah. Noah waited 100 years for the flood. During this process Noah was gaining experiences and character molding in building the Ark, he was not passive as there was a practical training that he was undergoing in waiting for the flood to come.

What about Joseph? Joseph waited for 13 years before the manifestation of his dream. This made Joseph trust God even more. The God who gave him the vision in the first place, and he knew that He alone was able to bring it to pass. This made Joseph more focused and ready to undergo the training that was packaged for him; and because God was in charge, his ordeals led to a glorious finish. Joseph's youthfulness did not influence him to be overwhelmed when he came face to face to youthful desires.

Occasionally, the Lord also reveals the end of our story to us before taking us through the times of trials like he did with Joseph. When God revealed the dreams of glory to Joseph, as a young excited boy, he was quick to inform the world by telling his vision to his family members without any caution. This, in turn, were the people programmed in his destiny to play the enemy roles that led Joseph to his height of prominence.

Joseph learned to seek and believe God's interpretation of dreams right from his youth even before being sold to traders and thrown into prison on a false accusation so that God might use him to interpret the dream of the cupbearer, who will later introduce him to the King that set Joseph over all the lands of Egypt. From his position of authority, he saved his people and his own family from famine (Gen. 37: 45).

All of the experiences gathered in the waiting room is what propels you and makes you be who you should be. Joseph learnt the Egyptian cultural way of life, language, food, understanding what their belief systems were. These experiences put together, prepared him to be launched out for his glorious destiny that God had given unto him. The waiting and training ground are the nesting seasons that comes with trials and temptations.

We should learn to accept God's training ground, don't resent God's training ground in any area that you are expecting your desire to be manifested. Most of the time, your personal ability to achieve a particular desire quickly does not necessarily mean it is God's will for your life, it might be permissive and not perfect will of God. The story of Sarah says more about this topic of temporary satisfaction that brings a long time of pain and sorrow (Genesis 16:2).

The Bible says "so she said to Abram, "the lord has kept me from having children. Go, sleep with my slave; perhaps I can build a family through her". Abram agreed to what Sarai said."

Abraham's action of laying with his wife's maid brought about the birth of a son not PROMISED by God. It might be momentarily fulfilling but ends up in regrets. I once had a relationship that was not carefully thought after, just prayed casually and I found myself in a pit that took only God to deliver me from. These are the kind of momentary satisfaction that makes one start all over again. Do not fall when the trying times come and do not give up in the face of temptation.

Amputated Training

BE AWARE YOU ARE WAITING

As humans, we are always under internal pressures to see the quick end of a trying period. This can cause a training leading to a bigger victory to be cut short. The training can be cut short when it is not yet your time. This for sure has the consequences that accompany a cut short training process.

Deciding to jump the gun is like saying I am tired and I want to do it in my own way. "There is a way which seems right unto a man, but the end, thereof, is the ways of death" (Prov.14:12). These days, men prefer to honor the counsel of men rather than God. This kind of fast track has led to destiny amputation. We all are on a journey of life which is not meant to be rosy at all times. Sometimes we see the good and the bad, and if it were not so, God wouldn't have told us in Isaiah 43: 2 about the fire we will go through and the sea, but also, the assurance He gave us that He is with us, we will not be burnt and we will not be drowned.

The fire and the sea in this scripture represent the situation and circumstances we go through in life that puts us in the waiting room as we experience the unpleasant moments in our life's journey.

The action you put in when you are terribly tired of your situation should be seriously weighed because the outcome of whatever it is at the end will either be positive or negative which will come back to you. The truth is that we should not allow our circumstance to dictate to us to the point we no longer hear God's voice.

Earlier I talked about my experience of when I was approaching age 30, how I thought all my age mates had all gotten married and I felt very uncomfortable with myself at this season of my life. It was difficult for me to hear God even when He was speaking, and I ended up allowing my age of getting older influenced me to take a major decision to get into a relationship that almost ruined my life.

BE AWARE YOU ARE WAITING

It took God's mercy to bring me out unharmed as I have mentioned earlier. If Abraham's wife Sarah had waited on God, she wouldn't have ended up with that momentary satisfaction that brought pain, not just to her that she had to send her maid away and no longer cared if the child survived, (Gen. 16:2), but also to all generation even to this day because of that action.

This single reason is why the God factor has to always be considered seriously. Gehazi was privileged to learn under Prophet Elisha, but impatience made him lose his glorious destiny and ended up being a leper and attracted a curse to his generation (2Kings 5:15-27). Preparation is an all-round balancing during the seasons of waiting.

Waiting is a process, you must understand that if a process is not completed, like a miscarried pregnancy, it will not mature and will likely lead to more sorrow. Waiting is God's way of training his children and helping them go through that fire of refinement so that when they come out, they will become as pure as gold. We must as God's children understand that waiting is part of being in God's vineyard, as it draws us closer to our maker.

Chapter Five

BE AWARE YOU ARE WAITING

n the third year of Cyrus king of Persia a thing was revealed unto Daniel, whose name was called Belteshazzar; and the thing was true, but the time appointed was long: and he understood the thing, and had understanding of the vision.

In those days I Daniel was mourning three full weeks.

I ate no pleasant bread, neither came flesh nor wine in my mouth, neither did I anoint myself at all, till three whole weeks were fulfilled.

Daniel 10:1-3

A pregnant woman is not scared of her bulging stomach, or that there is a movement inside her womb because she knows there is something inside that will come out after nine months. The pregnant woman knows she has to wait for nine months for her baby to be born. But if she does not know what pregnancy is or means, or take for example that she did not know she is pregnant and her stomach started swelling for some months, she will become uneasy and afraid, and probably engage in unsafe actions.

But when she comes to the realization and knowledge of what pregnancy means, or that she is pregnant, she will no longer be afraid. It will make her look a bit deformed and sometimes come with painful moments, but she will not be moved, because she knows why she is feeling that way and the right time will come for her to bring forth her baby.

Knowing and accepting the fact that you are in a season that will turn around to bring forth your desire, is enough assurance that gives you confidence through that season. As a child of God, you must remind yourself of the season that you are in, because knowing that you are in a season of waiting will help you. If you know you have to wait, you will make the decision to enjoy your life while you are waiting. Joel Osteen said, "why not be happy when God is in the process of changing things?"

The Shunammite woman was in a place of contentment in her situation when God remembered her through Elisha, Elizabeth the mother of John the Baptist was at peace with God in her situation and also Samson's parents. Just as a pregnant woman is forced to wait for nine months until delivery, so you must wait in your tough moment because sincerely, there is nothing you can really do to make it happen any faster, rather, to remind God of His promises through His word, divine revelations and prophecies you have gotten in this season.

Keep in mind, that true joy means to be free of worry and fear and reflects a state of contentedness that everything necessary is being taken care of. We might as well relax and enjoy our lives, knowing that at the appointed time God is going to bring His plans to pass.

After the troubles I went through about singlehood, God brought a responsible and committed man my way. In fact, it was at the time of finishing this book that I was restored to marriage. It was breakthrough after a season of making a bad choice, of being in a deceptive relationship. I now know that the truth, and it was that I ought to have waited. I am also lucky that God's grace saw me through even when I failed. You have to wait for God's timing and a turning point in your life.

Better to be matured in your Christian walk with God, irrespective of your past, He will do a new thing (Isaiah 43:19). When you come to this reality, it is a turning point in your life, it is an eye-opener. It makes waiting full of hope that will give you inner peace which will make that desire to manifest. Pray for your strength to be renewed, you will mount up with wings and not grow weary. In the book of Isaiah 40:31 The Bible says, "They that wait upon the Lord, shall renew their strength, they shall mount up with wings like eagles, they shall run and not be weary, and they shall walk, and not faint".

One thing is sure, that every child of God will fulfil their glorious destiny unless that one is not in alignment with God. The thoughts God has for you is for good and to bring you to your desired future (Jeremiah 29:11).

This is the assurance we have that sickness is unto healing, bareness is unto fruitfulness, and that stagnation is unto promotion. Turn up the light of God in you and begin to see Jesus through your seasons of discomfort. Christ in us is the hope of all glory, Hallelujah!

This will happen if only you yield to God and follow His direction for your life. When you know you are waiting for something and the one who asks you to wait is trustworthy, that makes waiting to be full of expectations and less worrisome; you put your faith in God's integrity to fulfil His word because He is too faithful to fail. According to the book of John 11:1-44, Jesus received a message that Lazarus was ill, and his two sisters were urgently seeking his help. Jesus told his followers; "this sickness will not end in death. No, it is for God's glory so that God's Son will be glorified through it."

Focus on His promises regarding what you are expecting. The Personality that promised you is not a man with any form of limitation (Numbers 23:19) (Matthew 7:11). He will not promise you and fail. The story of Hannah in the Bible who needed a child so desperately and who went to Shiloh to pour her heart to God will shed more light on God keeping to His promise.

You have to remember that Hannah had been going to Shiloh over the years, but this particular Shiloh season was her period of visitation irrespective of the irritating comments she got during her waiting seasons from people. She never allowed herself to give up on God. Job 14:14 "I Will Wait Until My Change Comes".

Hannah's faith was in action which made Eli pronounce the blessing upon her. Priest Eli prayed for her and gave her a word of assurance. She went home rejoicing believing it was done. This attitude made her not only to conceive but she had more than what she asked for.

In your waiting, always confess who you are in Christ Jesus. Some of us speak words contrary to our desire after we have prayed towards the direction of our expectation. You are believing God for children and at the same time saying negative things about children or rejecting other people's children coming around you.

This act can hinder your desire. Embrace children if that is your expectation, get a gift for your unborn children, make a sacrifice. So is waiting for a life partner to come; you must be praying for him or her, even before he finds you or you find her. In all of these, we have to be conscious in the area of our expected desire. Genesis 1:18, "And the Lord God said; it is not good that the man should be alone; I will make him a help meet for him". That is God's promise for those who are single and desire to be married. Always set your mind to victory.

Naomi and Ruth were aware of their waiting season and they were deliberate about what they wanted, and they were also conscious. In anticipation of what God was about to do in the life of Ruth, Naomi tutored Ruth in such a way that Boaz became Naomi's in-law by marrying Ruth (Ruth 2:4).

Esther and Mordechai also knew they were not in their glorious season, yet they were deliberate how they behaved and prepared for what they wanted. Mordechai told Esther not to disclose who she was and she obeyed all the instructions given to her, she went through the preparation stages and she became the wife of the King.

The different processes which were seen in their waiting season climaxed into the fulfilment of their glorious destiny. The Jews were delivered from death when Haman issued a decree to eliminate all the Jews in the entire province and Mordecai was remembered, he was honored for what was due to him that was denied of him over the years until the appointed time came. Even though Mordecai knew he ought to have been rewarded for saving the Kings life a long time ago, he was not in a hurry, he patiently and diligently waited for God's timing to intervene in his case.

Do you know you are waiting?

Martha and Mary had to be compelled to wait for Jesus' timing. Ordinarily, both sisters wanted their own timing because the situation seemed urgent and nothing was forthcoming. He wanted them to wait, to prove that He is the resurrection and the life! He needed their attention to be focused on Him alone. He needed to let them know and be aware they were waiting.

He wanted to show them and those that know their case that His Glory will be made manifest through the situation. He wanted them to enter into His rest and not panic. Beloved of God, having faith and focusing on Him is the option He wants you to choose. Scriptures opined that life and death are before you and I want you to choose life (Deuteronomy 30:19).

Choose faith instead of fear, God works with faith and the devil uses fear to hinder your blessings. "This day I call the heavens and the earth as witnesses against you that I have set before you life and death, blessings and curses. Now choose life, so that you and your children may live." (Deuteronomy 30:19).

Many don't act in the consciousness and expectation of waiting and forget themselves. Once I used to be very conscious of how I looked, I mean my physical appearance, but at a point, I stopped paying much attention to it. Sometimes I would wear unfashionable clothes which sometimes had inconsistent colour combinations or colour riot as some ladies would call it.

My pastor would encourage us young ladies to dress up! Look good! Be presentable! And tell us that knowing that we are waiting should bring us to the consciousness of preparation towards that desire. Nobody usually wants to associate with a shabby personality or a nonchalant attitude that is repelling. Knowing that you are waiting should tell from the way you speak positively and behave towards that which

you are expecting God to do.

Chapter Six

OVERCOMING IN WAITING

iving the life of an overcomer even in the face of tribulation is what I am preaching in this chapter, because It is important that you do not live a life of hopelessness when your hope is on God. You cannot live a life of feeling defeated when your victory is in Jesus Christ.

To live a life of an overcomer in your season of waiting means you must change your mentality concerning that situation and be positive; you must walk in obedient with God, knowing fully that the price has been paid. Psalm 119:11 says" Your word I have hidden in my heart, that I might not sin against You".

Now that you know you have overcome spiritually in the name of Jesus, then your physical life must tell it even though you are still in your waiting season. Even when it has not manifested physically, you must walk in the victory of what the scripture says concerning that matter, because if God be with you, no man can be against you. You are more than a conqueror in Christ Jesus.

The joy of walking with God through your seasons in life, either negative or positive, is that you are rest assured that you are not alone in the boat, this is the peace that surpasses any other. This is the time you should feel grateful.

Another thing you must also keep in mind is to help those that are in the same situation or waiting season as you. Just as you will not do to yourself, do not be judgmental over people going through tough seasons of their lives, even after you have come out of yours.

Importantly also, do not be anxious for anything, do not blame or accuse anybody of abandoning you, especially those you have helped in the past because it is only God that can help you. Men will forget your favour, but God cannot.

When Joseph was in prison, he interpreted a dream to the cupbearer which came to pass, and he pleaded with the cupbearer that he should remember him when he got his freedom. Eventually, the cupbearer forgot him, he forgot he was once a prisoner before he got his desired freedom. God had to orchestrate a circumstance that triggered the cupbearer to remember Joseph.

Joseph's interpretation of dreams was the talent that he used to the glory of God and the benefit of others. Beloved of God, it is in this trying times you must use your gift to the glory of God and the benefit of men. What will you interpret to them? Just like Joseph who interpreted dreams, use your gift to interpret God's love and God will use it to trigger more blessings for you. Let that situation in your past bring light to others in darkness (Romans 15:1).

We who are strong have an obligation to bear with the failings of the weak, and not to please ourselves. We should be able to share with others especially when we have received the Grace to pull through. Speak those words of encouragement that can help them as they go through their season, and you will find that it will also help you to cope.

Your joy of overcoming in waiting shouldn't just be your joy alone without touching and impacting lives. The experience in the prison should tell more of how you should have compassion for those who are there. The prison is not a pleasant place to be, especially mental prison; your freedom is restricted, your joy is tamed and so many things will cause you pain.

It takes the grace of God to bring one out of that shame, uncertainty and low self-esteem. So if you finally find a way to live victoriously even in your situation, share the testimony to boost the faith of others. Share with them who are still feeling hopeless, this is the only way our joy can be full. The victory gotten is what the book of Revelation chapter 12:11 is talking about that we overcame by the blood of the Lamb and by the word of our testimony. The testimony is very key to help others get their freedom to overcome in waiting seasons of their life.

I could remember when I was called upon to be a minister in my local parish when it was planted in 2013, this for me was a confirmation that God has heard my cry for mercy and that I am free from every accusation of the enemy, every guilt feeling and fault findings.

It was like the prodigal son coming to His father and he was celebrated. It was a turning point for me, a new dawn in the era of my destiny. I was so excited that I described that day as a day of leaping for Joy, like the one felt by baby Jesus and baby John when Mary met Elizabeth the mother of John (Luke 1:41). The Spirit of God embraced me and I was overjoyed.

So when you feel like you have sinned and come short of the glory of God, do not give up in living the life of grace. Continue to thank God for his forgiveness over your life, while also forgiving yourself. Because if you have not forgiven yourself, it is going to be a lot of challenge believing that God has forgiven you.

Even when you do not hear from God, whether directly or through the servants of God, you must know that he is faithful and just to deliver and forgive us of our sins.

Importantly, you must not forget the aspect of service. This is one aspect of waiting that even makes waiting very effective. Live in His vineyard because He is your father and is ready as always to draw you close no matter how far you have gone, like the prodigal son.

As long as you come back home and are ready to rededicate yourself to Christ, and wait upon the Lord to do His mighty works, your waiting season will be joyful, and the end of your waiting will be so glorious you will not be able to describe it.

To overcome is to change our mindset over the situation we are going through, by using the word of God as a compass to see through that circumstance. Even in the time when everything is tough, I mean the time of waiting, if you have the opportunity to be a blessing to others, do so.

It doesn't have to be financial, it may be a word of wisdom and encouragement, prophecy (if you have the gift of prophecy), or in whichever way that God has placed in your heart.

Joseph in the prison did not let the prison yard lock up his gifts. He did not allow his time of waiting to cloud his ability to dream dreams and he used his gift to the glory of God even in the prison. Beloved of God, show forth God's glory every time, even in your waiting and do not be afraid, because God Himself is with you always.

Below are some Biblical verses that can help you to overcome in your time of waiting.

Feel and Confess the Right Words always.

FACTS: THE OPPRESSION	SCRIPTURES	THE TRUTH! MY FAITH!	MY CONFESSION
STILL SINGLE?	**Isaiah 34:16**	Seek ye out of the book of the LORD, and read: no one of these shall fail, none shall want her mate: for my mouth it hath commanded, and his spirit it hath gathered them.	For the mouth of the Lord has spoken and his Spirit has gathered them saying, I will not fail, I will not lack my mate in Jesus' name...Amen
NO CHILDREN?	Exodus 23;26	None shall lose her young by miscarriage or be barren in your land; I will fulfill the number of your days. AMP.	I was given birth to by my parent and I must give birth to my children for the Lord says I will not be barren or

			lose my baby by miscarriage for He will fulfil the number of my days and perfect everything concerning me. Amen.
I AM SICK?	Isaiah 53:5	But he was wounded for our transgress-ions, he was bruised for our iniquities: the chastisement of our peace was upon him; and with his stripes we are healed. JKV.	But he was wounded for my transgressions, he was bruised for my iniquities, the chastisement of my peace was upon him, and with his stripes I am healed...Amen.
NOT HAPPY?	Nehemiah 8:10	Then he said unto them, Go your way, eat the fat, and drink the sweet, and send portions unto them for whom nothing is prepared: for this day is holy unto our LORD: neither be ye sorry; for the joy of the LORD is your strength. KJV.	I will eat, drink and give out to the needy in happiness, my days are holy for the Lord, no one will sorry or pity for me for the joy of the Lord is my strength...Amen.
THE SITUATION IS OVERWHELMING?	Job 14:14	If a man dies, shall he live again? All the days of my appointed time will I wait, till my change come. KJV.	Thank you Lord Jesus for giving me the Grace to wait for all days of my appointed time for

			my change, I can see all things are turning around for me in all aspects of my life...Amen.
TAKING LONGER THAN EXPECTED?	Proverb 23:18	For surely there is a latter end (a future and a reward), and your hope and expectation shall not be cut off. AMP.	I stand on the word of God and I declare that my hope and my expectation shall not be cut off...Amen.
FEELING OLD?	Isaiah 40:31	But they that wait upon the LORD shall renew their strength; they shall mount up with wings as eagles; they shall run, and not be weary; and they shall walk, and not faint. KJV.	Because I wait upon the Lord my strength is renewed, I am mounting up with wings as eagles, I will run and not be weary, and I will walk and not faint...Amen.
I am worried	1 Peter 5:7	Casting all your anxieties on him because he cares for you. ESV.	I cast all my anxieties to you Jesus for you care for me...Amen.
I feel discouraged	Deuteronomy 31:8	It is the Lord who goes before you. He will be with you; he will not leave you nor forsake	The Lord is going before me. He is with me; he will not leave me nor

		you. Do not fear or be dismayed. ESV.	forsake me. For I am not afraid or dismayed... Amen.

The FACT and the TRUTH

The 'fact' describes the situation you're going through, while the 'truth' is the living word of God that is contrary to the 'fact,' but provides a solution. It is your personal confession of the living word of God against that situation that will make the difference and bring forth your desired breakthrough.

You intentionally or consciously use the word of God through FAITH to combat that situation that is real in the physical but FAKE in the true sense of the word of God. God disapproved the enemy to prevail over you (Lamentations 3: 37)

Chapter Seven

WHAT TO DO WHILE WAITING

It is easy to lose one's self while waiting. It is easy to roll into a ball-like shape and wallow in depression, pain and anguish while going through the process of waiting. Many times, we want to stay in a state of nothingness because our expectations, our prayers and the needs we are asking from God are all slow in coming.

Don't just fold your hands and sit like someone who is carrying the entire weight of the world on his or her shoulders. God wouldn't want you to stay still and keep your life on a pause, He will want you to stand up and start developing yourself. While waiting on God to send that special package, you should do the following and adhere to them rigorously;

Pray

God's word opined that we should pray without ceasing. Praying is one of the most important actions you can engage in while you wait. Whether praying alone or involving others who are prayerful, the praying process is very important and helpful. Many things are possible when we stretch our faith, collaborate with other believers and open up to other people of faith.

In the book of 1 Peter 5:7, the word of God admonishes us to cast all our fears and anxiety upon Him because He cares so much about us. God is concerned about our needs and feelings. He wants to be right beside us as we take several intentional steps towards redemption.

Prayer and praying help us to build up our faith in God, grow spiritually and also develop spiritual capability and capacity. Sometimes we might not have the capacity and ability to be able to take and carry what God is sending towards us. Prayer and praying help us to develop and have the capacity to be able to take what God is sending to our path. Spiritual maturity and growth are enshrined in prayer and studying of God's word.

The Truth In God's Word

Courage, faith and hope are gotten from the undiluted word of God. While waiting in God, the word of God is the best friend to have while you go through the waiting season. Memorize scriptures, speak the word consistently on a daily basis, read Christian literature and allow the word to take root in your heart and bring forth fruit.

Waiting can be a tedious exercise and can be strenuous. Concentrating on the newness and the truth embedded in God's word will help you in making the best decisions and refuting the lies of the enemy. The word of God is the armour you need to face the issues you are facing. The word of God is like a combustion fuel which is necessary to energize us through the waiting period. It helps in building capacity and it teaches us everything which is associated with God.

Another critical advantage of God's word in our life while waiting is the strength to stand up against the enemy (Satan) and his lies. While waiting, there is a possibility of the devil inserting some sneaky lies into your heart (he is the father of all liars), based on certain weak points. The word of God helps in developing a shield to block the lies of the enemy from infiltrating our hearts.

While in the wilderness after Jesus Christ fasted for forty days and forty nights; the devil sneaked upon Him with his many lies and temptation but Jesus Christ dealt with the situation by using the word of God which was at his disposal. Jesus Christ had a weak point in that situation; He was hungry, tired and in need of food but at his physical weakened situation, the word of God was His strength, and all He needed to deal with the lies of the evil one.

While waiting, normalize studying God's word and hearing from God through the scriptures. Normalize yielding to God's directions and guard your heart with God's word, because what proceeds out of your heart are the issues of life.

List What God Has Done In Your Life

Naturally, while we wait our hearts are always in a haste to get the request we have made to God, in that process, the possibility of having a dampened faith occurs. Feeling like God has left you. Take a pen and a journal and make a list of what God has done in your life.

Listing the things which God has done in my life has helped in many ways. One of the major reasons for listing the blessings out is to boost your faith and to remember what God has done in the past. This helps in various ways.

List them down and you will be amazed at the number of blessings you will come up within a short period of time. Sometimes, I sit and make a mental list of the goodness of God in my life and just end up smiling.

A written list of God's blessings gives you the confidence and trust that God will do exceedingly, based on what He has promised. You can trust that the God who has helped you yesterday, is able and capable to help you today and in the nearest future.

Develop Yourself While Waiting

Many people become depressed, fixed at a place and even stop developing themselves because of their present situation. God's purpose for us is not to stay in a particular place week in and week out. Staying idle physically, spiritually, mentally and otherwise is not the will of God for His children. God wants us to develop various aspects of our lives as we wait.

Learn a skill, develop your social skills if you have none; develop the habit of reading both spiritual, educational and financial books. Read positive contents focusing on that thing you're expecting from God. Develop a good personality and attitude while waiting. Many a time we don't get what we are waiting for as quick as God would have liked us to have it simply because we don't have the right attitude.

A blog content by Beverly titled "On becoming the oil and wine" reads:

Patience is not the ability to wait alone but it is the ability to keep a good attitude while waiting. Waiting in God through patience helps in building the right attitude. A good attitude is developed while waiting and when waiting in the presence of God.

Accept You Are Running Your Own Race

One of the things the devil keeps inserting into our consciousness when we are waiting is trying to compare our situation with that of others, such as friends, church members, classmates, colleagues, siblings and people who were once in the same situation with us. As success 'haunts you', you are likely to start comparing yourself with other people. But you must remember that you are running your own race and must continually believe in God.

I shared my story about waiting for a life partner. I started listing out what other people who are in the same age range as I had accomplished. The devil started making comparisons and infusing certain thoughts in my head. It took God' grace to ignore him as I renew my mind with God's word.

You must know that your unveiling season is different from others' because you are unique and peculiar. You must know that you have your own unique gifts which the world will see when the appointed time comes. Run your own race, accept your situation is temporary and believe God to open doors which were made specifically for you.

Reflect on Where You Began

While in the waiting process, we might think we have not been moving forward despite the time frame. Taking reflection of where you began is a very good action to see that God has been faithful, and He will continue to be faithful and will continue with what He has started in your life. When you reflect on where you are coming from and where you are now, you will find out that you're making incredible strides on getting to that point you want to get to.

You will find out that you didn't get to where you are by accident but by conscious efforts and the grace of God. Waiting for your special package doesn't have to be a sad, depressing and a dreadful period of time. Waiting shouldn't be an excuse to be a rock in a wilderness covered with grass and does not move but stay stagnant. Waiting shouldn't be an excuse to slow down. Waiting can become an opportunity to soar higher and develop the different aspects of your life and be ready to embrace your miracles.

Fuel Your Passion

When women, usually in rural areas of Nigeria, want to cook with their local firewood method, they start by arranging the dry woods, insert the igniter and allow the yellow flames to blossom. For the fire to continue to blossom and spread its beautiful yellow flames, the woman will continue inserting dry firewood, kerosene, plastics and continue fanning the flame.

She will continue with the various actions until she is done cooking the food (trophy). Taking a leaf from the process of using firewood to cook, we will find out that we can make use of the 'firewood' in our waiting situation.

Fuel your passion, exhaust and embrace every opportunity to expand your passion. If it is an academic scholarship you are waiting for, take classes, and take developmental examinations and tests, which are focused on your course of study. Read academic journals and continue fanning the flames of your passion.

God wants to see that you are really interested in that passion and what you are waiting for. Pour gasoline to your fire, pour water to that growing plant, study to show yourself approved, cloth yourself to meet that expectation, learn how to talk and communicate adequately, eat the right way, walk the right way, open yourself to facilitate relationships, go out on dates, leave that comfort zone and always try to be the real you.

Other actions to take while waiting include the following: celebrate your little wins, meditate on God's promises, study the different names of God and talk to your spiritual mentor or pastor, sometimes exalt yourself, speaking to oneself is considered therapeutic and be among brethren in service.

I am believing this aspect of this book is able to gear you up for what's ahead as you prepare to be launched to the next level of victory in Jesus name.

Chapter Eight

READY TO BE LAUNCHED OUT

What should you do when launched out into your divine destiny? Live a life of expectation. You must be full of expectations (Jeremiah 29:11). I came across this statement of expectancy I think will be great to share;

To expect is to look forward to something, regarding it as very likely to happen. It means anticipating the occurrence or the coming of something. It has to do with your attitude. And all of us know that like an aeroplane, our attitude determines our altitude. Your atmosphere is closely linked to your attitude. Your atmosphere is the mood, the influence, the environment you surround yourself in. An atmosphere without expectation will kill your dreams. It destroys the hope that is within you. An atmosphere of expectation is required for supernatural and divine intervention in your affairs and your life.

Expectation is the breeding ground for Miracles. Let me say here, faith without expectation is not faith enough. If you get into a bus or you are travelling, your expectation will always be that you must get to your destination.

When you live in expectation there will be a feeling of peace and contentment in that situation. You will have inner joy, favor and goodness gravitating towards you; speaking positively towards that expectation as though it has manifested is a great act of faith (Romans 4:17). It focuses on calling those things which are not as if they were.

My neighbor was arrested at his place of work for what he knew nothing about. It took us four weeks to work out the process of getting him out, and the actual culprit was also arrested. He shared his ordeal with us of what he went through in the prison.

He said by the second week in the prison, he felt he had been totally forgotten and abandoned by friends, neighbors and relatives. But that when it came to the third week, he saw an unusual light that focused on him, that attracted favor from fellow prisoners who suddenly made him their head; reporting to him and taking counsel from him.

He said it didn't end there, that a divine word came to him that he will be leaving there soon. The prison warders in fact suddenly took interest in him and were always checking up on him and giving him preferential treatment from the rest. According to him, he said he knew that God had stepped into his case, and the mindset alone changed the entire atmosphere.

It wasn't long after that he was eventually released. In the name of Jesus, every prison you are in right now, I declare you are coming out with your breakthrough, miracles and expectations! You have a God who is in that battle fighting for you and you need to hold your peace (Exodus 14:14). Your story is your glory in disguise (Isaiah 54:1-3)

Paul and Silas in the prison invoked this atmosphere of joy by praising God in dancing, clapping and singing, knowing well that God was with them and that they will not be forsaken. Acts 16:25-26 tells us that the prison doors were flung open on their own accord, isn't that great? Just like Elisha stepped into the situation of the Shunammite woman by the power of God.

When the angel told Elizabeth, she will carry a baby, at a point in her life she no longer worried about having children. This indeed is when God steps in to take Glory for Himself. It's all about God's Glory. We are clay and He is the potter who shapes us to His desired Will. He owns the times and seasons in His hands. Enter into His rest and be ready to be launched out.

Your season will surely come. God is saying have you not heard what I will do? I AM making a way in the wilderness, springing forth water in the desert, making the blind to see again, bringing money from the fish's mouth, making the axe to float again, raising dry bones to life, parting the red sea, shutting the mouth of the lions and thundering against the adversaries of your destiny. The blood of Jesus has blotted out your transgressions, now your mistakes and errors are forgotten? He is the same yesterday today and forever! This is the caliber of the God we serve.

Because you waited, trusting God through the process, you will have more than what you deserve in Jesus name, Amen!

I cried as I wrote this chapter of this book, not because I was emotional, depressed or tired, but for the truth that you and I are encouraged to free ourselves from the lies of the devil we were once deceived by, knowing so much that nothing will separate us from His love, for us, this is the truth that God has established! He is with you in that boat of life! He does not leave His own! His eyes watch over you!

As you look up to Him, your face will radiate His Glory! He is the lifter of your head! No weapon formed against you shall prosper! All authority has been given to you! He is with you fully.

No worries but tears of Joy fill my heart in worship of Him and His miraculous ways. Know that your expectation will come to pass as you pull through He will come through to you. You are being launched out for the right purpose and it is always in God's plan for your destiny that today and this moment is going to come. This moment serves a great purpose so you must not abuse it.

Your destiny is very important to God, so do not assume that the difficult period is God abandoning you. No, rather it is God launching you fully into the active service of living your destiny and purpose. Every fiber of your difficult moment matters to your destiny. God has not left you; he has only launched you. When a father sends his child to school, he does not sit with that child in class, no.

He launches the child into a world of testing and examining so that the child will be ripe for the greater glory to come. God has launched you, no matter what it is you are going through now, know that it is because you have been launched, and this time is important for your destiny. This is why you must wait upon the lord without an iota of doubt.

Chapter Nine

PREPARATION FOR YOUR GLORIOUS DESTINY

There is a shining waiting after your trying times have passed. Brace up and walk through all your valley situations with confidence in God. Preparation is getting ready to be trained, to be conscious, to learn, to fit into, to be aware of and to be deliberately looking forward to receiving. It is the season which precedes restoration.

Preparation is simply getting ready to receive that which you have been waiting for; it is the period of time which comes before the fulfilment of the manifestation of your expectation in the season of waiting.

Preparation is a victory mentality or mindset to win. Winter is a dormant season, it is a time when the trees become bare and most of the grass, plants and flowers die off, but it is also a time of preparation as roots and tree saps respond to soil and temperature changes to prepare for the growth that comes in the spring. The same way, you and I go through preparation seasons.

These are the reasons God may seem to us to be silent and distant and far away from us. Many times, it may seem as if He has abandoned us, but it is the winter season that we must use to prepare ourselves. It is the season when it seems as if our dreams and visions are dimmed without any form of illumination.

When we find ourselves in this quagmire or dry period where nothing exciting is happening, but it doesn't really mean nothing is happening. The dry season is a season, the period of time when our faith is being built as we prepare for harvest. The time frame where we learn, unlearn and relearn certain aspects about God, faith, ourselves, our community and other people. The waiting season is a time when we are beaten into shape like the crude gold which has to pass through intense heat from a furnace to be reborn and come out glowing.

A lot has to happen on the inside of us before we are ready to handle the future God has prepared for us. Just as winter prepares plants and trees for warmer weather, so also waiting helps our inner character to be developed. Beautiful on the inside and outside, that is God's desire for us. Although we usually focus more on the preparation for the outside forgetting to build the inside.

The waiting season doesn't make you unqualified for God's blessings because you are blessed already, but His will and purpose must be accomplished to build the inside so that we can be beautiful on the outside. Strength and strong character are essential for withstanding storms that come during seasons of growth and harvest. We all go through seasons of waiting. The Bible tells us of how Jesus grew and increased in wisdom, stature, and in favor with God and man before He was fully ready to make a global impact in His ministry (Luke 2: 52). He needed to be prepared for His glorious destiny that was to come.

During your period of waiting, examine your motives and let it be in alignment with God's purpose for your life. Get out of your comfort zone, the place of total relaxation and embrace discipline like the spiritual army God says you are. My local parish pastor and his wife once attested to my obedience to serve. Sincerely this was a conscious and deliberate decision I had to take, to help me grow in my walk with God, engaging my mind with the things that matter most to my soul.

It has made seasons of waiting less depressing and therapeutically restored my confidence that was shattered years back due to decisions that were not carefully examined, that led me into a bad relationship.

The waiting period can be very useful in helping us to deal with the experience of several wrong decisions. I found out that working and putting conscious energy in working for and with God is making me a better person, just like the raw gold which goes through intense heating.

Henri Nouwen said in his words: "… recognize, believe that the many unexpected events are not just disturbing interruptions of our projects, but the way in which God molds our hearts and prepares us"

Frank Damazio, in his book "From Barrenness to Fruitfulness" said, "Usually we don't ask for brokenness but God in His infinite wisdom sees to it that we go through what is necessary"

According to Dr Charles Stanley;

We all know what it means to be broken, to be shattered, to feel as if our entire world has fallen apart, we all have times in our lives when we don't want to raise our head off the pillow, and when we feel certain that the tears will never stop flowing. Brokenness is often accompanied by emptiness, a void that cannot be filled, and sorrow that cannot be comforted, a wound for which there is no healing balm. We are being prepared in our impatience to succeed; we overlook the qualifications for success. We may feel ready for a certain task, but God keeps the door closed. Instead, He has us doing some boring and inane (and irrelevant) task completely unrelated to our purpose but all along God is preparing our character to what He knows is ahead.

God wants to use you to change the world, but first He wants to change you and illuminate your heart. While we wait, we know God created each of us to do specific things (Ephesians 2:10). However, God seldom puts us immediately into the place He ultimately desires us to serve. Service is an action which is aimed at intense spiritual growth and I found out when I gave myself totally to the service of the kingdom via my local parish.

There is a reason to be prepared in the waiting room. A bride that is being dressed up to be presented to his groom need to take all the beauticians' instructions, so that like Esther, for her to be pleasing and acceptable to her groom who has been waiting to behold his beautiful bride. So also, it is for us, waiting makes us appreciate that which we receive,

Bongos Ikwue sang "nothing good comes easy" and this is very true. There must be action and preparedness to bring forth that breath-taking desire you have been waiting for, mental preparedness, spiritual preparedness, physical preparedness, emotional preparedness and of course financial preparedness is needed.

The world cup 2018 event that was hosted by Russia, even though they hosted it, their teams still had to engage in long and tough preparation before they were launched out to represent their country. "No preparation No presentation" Elohortex.

Wayne Stiles Tweeted a Quote which said "While you count the fishes, our character remains more important to God than our accomplishments", although, for us, it's usually the opposite. Without godly character, our abilities and accomplishments are undermined and the purpose for which God created us is hindered.

The waiting room is called life. You may have your appointment scheduled on how things should go, but it's totally God's discretion when it is time. Proverbs 16:1 the preparations of the heart belong to man, but the answer of the tongue is from the Lord. Joseph in the Bible went through all the preparation in the waiting room for several years before God brought Him out to fulfil his glorious destiny.

The vision that was revealed years back to him began to manifest after 13years of waiting through test and trials. As you count those fishes, be assured that God has plans for you and that His plans for you include preparation and waiting. Your glorious destiny has now been activated and launched.

Do not be afraid of the challenges ahead, but wait on the Lord for he is ready to bring your victory to pass. Can you see it? Can you smell it? Can you feel it? Yes, that's your victory. It is here already, claim it!

Chapter Ten

STAY WITH GOD THE DESTINY SUSTAINER

The Parable of the Prodigal Son is one of the parables of Jesus which appears in Luke 15:11–32. The prodigal son returned home empty-handed to beg his father to accept him back as a servant.

The prodigal son understood that he has missed his part in life and that he needed to reconnect to his father who can help him restate his destiny part. his sustainer was his father, that without him he could do nothing, and that informed his decision to go back home.

He knew it was in his father's bosom that he could be secured, directed aright, be blessed, be forgiven and forever enjoy. Beloved of God, stay connected to God always, staying with the destiny sustainer is what God requires of us. He is always near if we are ready to draw closer to him and connect to him as our only sustainer.

The more your desires are being met, you should be fully aware that the enemy will continue to plot higher means to want to get to you and your blessings. Your glory becomes very attractive for the devil to want to prey on and destroy. Job was once a victim of this circumstances but God in His infinite mercy prevented the devil from tampering with his life.

As children of God, we must not be ignorant of the devices of the enemy. The devil is always looking for whom to devour irrespective of your righteous state. Remember the agenda of the enemy is three-fold, to kill, to steal and to destroy. you know after waiting for so long to get your blessing to manifest, you wouldn't want to be careless about how it can be sustained. God is your only sustainer and your defense.

When the enemy comes like a flood, the Spirit of the living God will lift up a standard against them.

Isaiah 59:19 (paraphrased)

Sanballat and Tobias were not happy over the move of Nehemiah to rebuild the falling walls of Jerusalem. So, they devised means to amputate this plan, but thanks be to God that Nehemiah knew that God was with him and he did acknowledge this truth in the place of prayer, fasting and faith by taking action and getting the people to work harder because victory was sure.

In Numbers 23:23, Balak and Balaam wanted to pull down God's people, the Israelites. They desperately acted on this evil plot and tried to make sure that they succeed in their plans. This was as a result of the blessings of the Israelites who were waxing stronger as they progressed in life. Not that the children of Israel did anything wrong to Balaam. He was not just happy that they were enjoying dominion.

Our confidence is that when you are in Christ Jesus there is no condemnation that will prevail even if they try. (Romans 8:1)

If God can know whatever passes through the path of the seas, you that is the work of His hands, he sees you and will work out your success plans. He is the only one who can sustain every good gift because He adds no sorrow to it.

Staying with God after getting that which you desire is very important; many people have missed this point in their journey in life. The prodigal son realized this truth in his life that the only person he could feel safe with, for his destiny to be restored and sustained, was his father. This was why he took the bold step of faith to go back to his father. In many cases, we tend to forget

God quickly after getting what we want and we are also quick to desire for more.

The story of the ten lepers in the Bible talks about this; how ten people were healed but only one, remembered to come back again to thank the source of his help (Luke 17:15-16). Your thanksgiving should be continuous, never stop thanking God who is the source of your breakthrough, and He alone can sustain what He had given you if you stay connected to Him.

Our help is in the name of the Lord who made the heavens and the earth. God is our destiny sustainer; we are engraved in the palm of His hands. This realization is what will make you sustain what you have received from above to have no sorrow in it.

We should come to this truth that the mercy of God endures forever (Psalm 136). As children of the Most High, our Father is always ready to receive any of His own that comes back to Him, no matter what has happened. This is not to say that we should continue in sin for His grace to abound, the Bible says 'God forbid'.

I have written this book because I cannot forget that in my sojourn, lost in my depression, frustration and playing blame games, I drew far from God; as a result, like the case of the prodigal son my case only grew worse. But once I looked up and repositioned my mind to allow the word of God to grow in my heart, God in His mercy showed me compassion and accepted me back.

No wonder God empowered me with His wisdom and grace to bring this book to reality by fulfilling in my life His word in Psalm 34:5, made my face to shine and radiate with His glory.(paraphrased)

Beloved of God your waiting time is not the time to grieve or sorrow and lose hope, otherwise, the enemy will believe they have gained victory over your life. Instead, our waiting time is the time to glory in the one that has launched us, that is guiding us and is available to sustain us. Do not rely on a man because they will fail you.

Rely on God only and always, because in him you have rest and hope. He is sufficient enough for you, no matter what you are going through. Waiting on the Lord is a must for every Christian especially when they are going through difficult times.

In the time frame between waiting and actualization, you must understand that preparation, training and planned actions must be carried out to make us better believers. Hold the victory of God in your heart as you are launched into your destiny. Remember, when your hope is built on nothing else but the love of God, victory is sure.

Chapter Eleven

MYSTERY OF GOD'S FAITHFULNESS

He answered and said unto them, because it is given unto you to know the mysteries of the kingdom of heaven, but to them it is not given.

Matthew 13:11

Even the mystery which hath been hid from ages and from generations, but now is made manifest to his saints.

Col 1:26

God demands from us total trust in Him/His words irrespective of our circumstances. He wants "TRUST" from you, a total reliance upon Him! He is the truth of the scripture, and in it, He spells out how well He needs everyone to rely upon scriptural truth totally.

Definition And Mystery Of God's Faithfulness

The word "faithful' connotes true or trustworthy in the performance of duty, the fulfilment of promises or obligations etc. These promises are the believer's focus in the time of waiting.

Different words describe faithful, including constant, loyality, stability, dependability, devotion, long-continued, steadfast, fidelity, infallibility, true to facts, trusted, and reliability. Interestingly, all these words are the attributes of God.

Moreover, when we say God is faithful, it means that we can trust Him, rely on Him, wait on Him, depend on Him totally and without reservation and that He will do what He says He will do. He is constant and consistent and does not change.

There failed not ought of any good thing which the LORD had spoken unto the house of Israel; all came to pass.

Joshua 21:45

Change is the only thing that is constant in life, but God is the only one that does not change. Deuteronomy 32:40 says, "For I lift up my hand to heaven, and say, I live forever." Also, Proverb 24:21 instructs that, "My son, fear thou the LORD and the king: and meddle not with them that are given to change." Then, Malachi 3:6 says, "For I am the LORD, I change not; therefore, ye sons of Jacob are not consumed."

Fatigue, wariness and so on make man change, but God is not subject to stress nor weakness. Isaiah 40:28 tells us that, "Hast thou not known? hast thou not heard, that the everlasting God, the LORD, the Creator of the ends of the earth, fainteth not, neither is weary? there is no searching of his understanding."

Heb. 13:8 as well says, "Jesus Christ the same yesterday, and today and forever."

Attributes Of God's Faithfulness

1.	*God is faithful to Himself by His attributes*

This is the attribute that qualifies other attributes, including love, holy, merciful, and divine. II Tim 2:13 says, "if we believe not, yet he abideth faithful, he cannot deny himself"

2.	*God is faithful to eternity*

Eternity is the age of God. Isa 57:15 tells us that, "For thus saith the high and lofty one that inhabiteth eternity, whose name is Holy: I dwell in the high and holy place...."

3.	*God is faithful to His people*

He demonstrates this through covenant. Gen 9:13 says, "I do set my blow in the cloud and it shall be for a token of a covenant between me and the earth." Deut. 7:9 also says, "Know therefore that the Lord, thy God, he is God the faithful God, which keepeth covenant and mercy with them that love him and keep his commandment to a thousand generations."

Then, Ps 50:5 says, "Gather my saints unto me; those that have made a covenant with me by sacrifice."

4.   *God is faithful to His promises*

For as the rain cometh down, and the snow from heaven, and returneth not thither, but watereth the earth, and maketh it bring forth and bud, that it may give seed to the sower, and bread to the eater: So shall my word be that goeth forth out of my mouth: it shall not return unto me void, but it shall accomplish that which I please, and it shall prosper in the thing whereto I sent it.

Is. 55:10-11

5.   *His promises are His prophecies*

God is not a man, that he should lie, neither the son of man, that he should repent, hath he said, and shall he not do it? or hath he spoken, and shall he not make it good?

Num 23:19

Heaven and Earth shall pass away; but my words shall not pass away.

Matt 24:35

For the mountain shall depart, and the hills be removed but my kindness shall not depart from thee, neither shall the covenant of my peace be removed, saith the Lord that hath mercy on thee.

Isa 54:10

6. *God is faithful to His Purpose*

His purpose is communicated to us in His words/promises.

For I know the thought that I think towards you saith the Lord, thoughts of peace and not of evil, to give you an expected end.

Jer 29:11

7. *God is faithful to His pronouncement*

His pronouncements are the revelations of His judgement. Heb 2:2 says, "For if the word spoken by angels was steadfast and every transgression and disobedience received a just recompense of reward." Also read the following: Ezek 3:18, Ezek: 18:20

8. *God is faithful to His plan and programs*

The secret things belong to God. His plans are embedded in the prophecies and His sacred words but concealed.

Deut. 29:29 says, "It is the glory of God to conceal a thing but the honour of kings is to search out a matter. Read Prov. 25:2 also.

Mystery Of His Faithfulness

The mystery of God's faithfulness is embedded in the difference between plan and purpose. When we wait on God, we are waiting for the end (purpose), which is the ultimate expectation.

A plan is a definite route to accomplish something God had planned for mankind, while purpose means a plan with no set route. The "how," most time, is missing. A route can be adjusted to circumstances. An example of a plan is seen when the scripture said a virgin shall conceive is one of the routes to achieve our salvation. Note that God's purpose is still to have mankind live in paradise forever but Adam's sin destroyed the easy route, so God adjusted the plan.

Plan is a drawing showing technical details of a building, machine and so on, with unwanted details omitted and often using symbols rather than phrases.

On the other hand, a purpose is an object to be reached, a target, an aim, a goal.

While you are waiting on God, you are waiting for God's manifestation (purpose, target, goal).

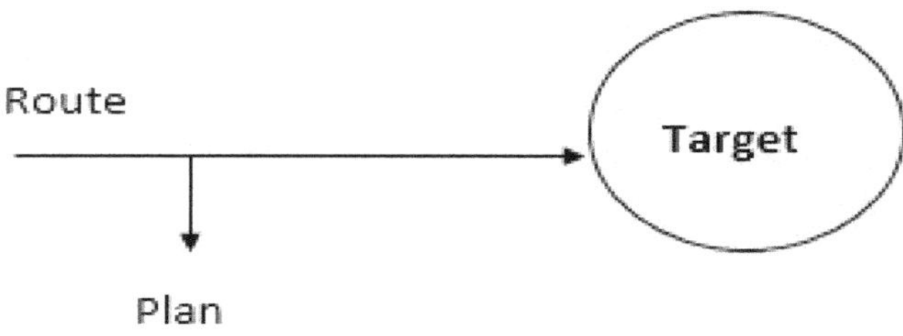

God, in most cases, does not reveal His plans, but gives us His purpose and many times, because of our limited human understanding, we cannot comprehend His purpose. Consequently, this makes us doubt him like Zechariah did and committed the sin of unbelief.

Knowing His plan (the explanation of how He would achieve the purpose) is crucial, but God has sovereignty taking this away from man. Instead, He proves His reliability to us!

For this missing plan, He demonstrates his faithfulness which is the compensation given to man for the missing plans in the architecture of his purpose. The plan is the missing part of the puzzle, concealed from the world but revealed only to his people at the place of waiting.

This is the missing code that the enemy is ever looking for to unlock God's plan. Up till today, interestingly, this missing code is what is making Lucifer run mad, aimlessly. Ps. 103:7 says, "He made known his ways (plans) to Moses, His acts (purpose) to the children of Israel."

What the enemy is looking for is the code. So, the only way Lucifer could compensate himself is by trial and error. Acts 1:7 says, "And he said unto them. It is not for you to know the times or the seasons, which the father hath put in his own power."

The plans are the hidden wisdom that devil cannot unravel. It is sacred; you cannot get it except in the waiting room where lies your victory. Such sacred information will only be given to the proved children of God.

But we speak the wisdom of God in a mystery, even the hidden wisdom, which God ordained before the world unto our glory. Which none of the princes of this world knew. For had they know it, they would not have crucified the Lord of glory.

1Cor. 2:7-8

The reason for the lack of perfect understanding of God's promises or the validity is because man does not have explanations for the way it should happen. We imagine things from human understanding and perspective, but the things of God are for spiritual sons of God. Unfortunately, whatever the mind of man is unable to process, he calls it foolishness like in the age of reason.

Because the devil does not understand the plan of bringing Christ to the world, he only knew the purpose. He, therefore, tried to block every assumed avenue through conspiracy. When he eventually realized that Christ had been born, he decided, by trial and error, to destroy all the newly born children. Matt. 2:16.

Till the rapture, Lucifer will continue to grope in darkness; he can never understand God's way/plans. He does not have the Holy Spirit, so he can only eavesdrop into the believer's conversation to tap into some mysteries.

In Acts 1:7, our Lord Jesus confirms it that God's plan is exclusive to God alone because knowing the times and season is like giving you the entire blueprint or plan of God to show you "the how long" and "when" the kingdom would be restored. This is exclusive to God alone.

Demonstration of His Faithfulness

According to Heb 6:16-20, we understand that men generally swear by him who is infinitely greater than themselves, and an oath to confirm what is promised or asserted usually puts an end to all contradiction.

God has therefore proved his faithfulness through an oath for you to trust Him. He accomplished this in a number of ways:

a. *By himself*

Gen 22:16 says, "And said, by myself I sworn, saith the Lord for because thou hast done this thing, and has not withheld thy son, thine only son."

b. *By His great name*

Jer. 44:26 says, "Therefore hear ye the word of the Lord, all Judah that dwell in the Land of Egypt; Behold I have sworn by my great name, saith the Lord, that my name shall no more be named in the mouth of any man of Judah in all the land of Egypt, saying the Lord God liveth.

c. By His life

Amos 6:8 says, "The Lord God hath sworn by himself, saith the Lord the God of hosts, I abhor the Excellency of Jacob, and hate his palaces; therefore, will I deliver up the city with all that is therein."

d. By His holiness

We find this in Amos 4:2 which says, "The Lord God hath sworn by his holiness that, lo, the days shall come upon you that he will take you away with hooks and your posterity with fishhooks."

e. By the pride of Jacob

In Amos 8:7, the scripture says, "The Lord hath sworn by the Excellency of Jacob surely, I will never forget any of their works."

f. By His right hand and mighty arm

Isa 62:8 says, "The Lord hath sworn by his right hand and by the arm of his strength, surely, I will no more give the corn to be meat for thine enemies; and the sons of the stranger shall not drink thy wine, for the which thou hast laboured."

God did all these to prove the immortality of His counsel/purpose (Ps 33:11, Dan 6:26). So, you can be sure that your victory is guaranteed in your waiting. Tell your soul like the Psalmist said: My soul, wait thou only upon God; for my expectation is from him. He only is my rock and my salvation (Psalm 62:5-8).

Always bear in mind that God's faithfulness is what sustains the wheat in the midst of the tares.

9 789785 664133